Dedication

"The first person to enter Paradise is Fatimah"

- The Holy Prophet, Muhammed.

I dedicate this book to Fatimah Zahra,
the daughter of Prophet Muhammed.
I pray this humble contribution will
earn me the honour of her intercession.

Hadith Al Kisa

The Event of the Cloak

(Colourful Children's Version)

By

R Mughal

Foreword

Let our sincere intentions be to teach our children

such that they ponder

over their faith and their actions,

and what comes from it.

Acknowledgements

All praise is for Almighty God, without his providence

nothing can be conceived or achieved.

Thank you to everyone who played

an active part in supporting this venture.

My son Muhammed,

without you this would

not have been possible.

You are my best friend and my small taste of paradise.

Welcome to my house!

My name is Fatimah Zahra.

I have a special surprise for you.

I'm going to tell you about my father, Muhammad,

and the cloak called the Kisa.

Let's read on.

I'm really excited for you to learn about it, too.

One day my father, Muhammad (the Messenger of

Allah),

came to my house.

"Assalaamu alayki, ya Fatimah," he said.

"Alaykas salaam," I replied, politely.

"O, Fatimah, please bring me the Kisa

and cover me with it," he requested.

After covering my father, I looked at his face.

It was glowing like the moon, so full of grace!

Then a little while later, my son, Hasan, arrived.

"Assalaamu alayki, ya Umma."

"Alaykas salaam, my darling," I replied.

"I smell something beautiful and pure,

like the nice scent of my

grandfather...for sure," said Hasan, with a big smile.

So, Hasan joined my father under the Kisa.

Soon after, my son, Hussayn, arrived.

"Assalaamu alayki, ya Umma."

"Alaykas salaam, my darling," I replied.

"I smell something beautiful and pure,

like the nice scent of

my grandfather...for sure," said Hussayn, with a big

smile.

So Hussayn too, joined my father under the Kisa.

Then came Ali, my husband and my father's cousin.

"Assalaamu alayki, o daughter of the Messenger of Allah."

"Alaykas salaam, Ameerul Mu'mineen," I replied.

"I smell something beautiful and pure,

like the nice scent of my cousin

...for sure," said Ali, with a big smile.

So, Ali too, joined my father under the Kisa.

I then peered under the cloak.

"Assalaamu alaykum, my father.

Can I please join you all under the Kisa?"

"Yes, of course, my darling.

YOU are a part of me, Fatimah," he replied.

My father, Muhammad, was so happy,

and being the Messenger, he spoke to Allah!

"My Ahlal Bayt are under this special cloak.

O Allah, please keep them safe and Al-Tahira."

"O Muhammed, I made everything

in the heavens and the earth,

For you Five Ahlal Kisa!" replied Almighty Allah.

The angel Jibraeel heard Allah's voice and asked,

"Who are these special five people under the Kisa?"

"They are the family of Fatimah:

Her father, Muhammad;

Her husband, Ali;

And her sons, Hasan and Hussayn," replied Allah.

"They are the Ahlal Bayt of Tahira."

Jibraeel was so excited and quickly

rushed to Fatimah's house.

He, too, wanted to join the Ahlal Bayt of Tahira.

And so he, too, sat under the Kisa!

"I wonder what this means...," said

Ali Ameerul Mu'mineen.

"Why did our family gather like this

under this cloak, the Kisa?" he asked.

"Allah has brought us together today,

under this Kisa to make us

the Ahlul Bayt of Tahira," replied Muhammad.

"What an amazing and kind Lord he is!

From now on...whenever anyone feels

sad or alone, or really wish for something

they want, remember this event and ask Allah for His

help! Allah will send his angels to pray

for them, and take care of them all!"

"WOW, how wonderful!" replied

Ali Ameerul Mu'mineen.

"Now that is a special surprise

from Almighty Allah—not just for us, but for

EVERYBODY!

What a kind Lord!"

So, there you are Children!

What started with my father and the Kisa,

Made us Ahlal Bayt of Tahira because of

what was said by Almighty Allah:

إِنَّمَا يُرِيدُ اللَّهُ لِيُذْهِبَ عَنكُمُ الرِّجْسَ أَهْلَ الْبَيْتِ وَيُطَهِّرَكُمْ تَطْهِيرًا

(33:33)

("Inna Maa yuree dul Allahu Li yudhhibah an kum rijsa Ahlu Bayti wayou

Tahhira kum Tat heeraa")

"Allah only wishes to remove uncleanness from you,

o members of the (Prophet's) household,

and to purify you completely" *(Tanzil.net Translation by Maududi)*

Please share this special message from

Lady Fatimah Zahra

with all your family and friends!

 @FourteenFiveBooks

 @Fourteen5Books

Word List:

Ahlal-Bayt - Term to describe the "People of the House" or "Family of the House". In this amazing event, it shows us who these people were

Ahlal Kisa - People of the Cloak or Blanket

Ameerul Mu'mineen - The title given to Ali for being the best of leaders for all the faithful Muslims

Jibraeel - Arabic name for the Angel Gabriel

Kisa - The Special Blanket or Cloak that was used by Muhammed

Messenger of Allah - Muhammed, who passed on the message directly from Almighty Allah to everyone else

Prophet - a person who is granted a special power by God that allows him to talk directly to God

33:33 - This refers to the Surah (chapter) and Verse number in the holy book, the glorious Quran.

Tahira - Pure, Clean, and free from that feeling of being unclean

Umma - Arabic word which means mother

You can also order from our UK based Webstore

Scan QR Code

FOURTEEN FIVE BOOKS

COLOURFUL ISLAMIC NARRATIONS FOR LITTLE MONSTERS

Fourteen Five Books is a part of Fourteen Five Limited

www.fourteenfiveltd.co.uk

Thank You!

Made in the USA
Middletown, DE
23 September 2018